Library Technology
R E P O R T S
Expert Guides to Library Systems and Services

Mobile Technology in Libraries

David Lee King

ALA TechSource
alatechsource.org

American Library Association

Library Technology REPORTS

ALA TechSource purchases fund advocacy, awareness, and accreditation programs for library professionals worldwide.

Volume 57, Number 2
Mobile Technology in Libraries
ISBN: 978-0-8389-4822-4
DOI: https://doi.org/10.5860/ltr.57n2

American Library Association
225 N. Michigan Ave., Suite 1300
Chicago, IL 60601-7616 USA
alatechsource.org
800-545-2433, ext. 4299
312-944-6780
312-280-5275 (fax)

Advertising Representative
Patrick Hogan
phogan@ala.org
312-280-3240

Editor
Patrick Hogan
phogan@ala.org
312-280-3240

Copy Editor
Judith Lauber

Production
ALA Production Services

Cover Design
Alejandra Diaz and ALA Production Services

Library Technology Reports (ISSN 0024-2586) is published eight times a year (January, March, April, June, July, September, October, and December) by American Library Association, 225 N. Michigan Ave., Suite 1300, Chicago, IL 60601-7616. It is managed by ALA TechSource, a unit of the publishing department of ALA. Periodical postage paid at Chicago, Illinois, and at additional mailing offices. POSTMASTER: Send address changes to Library Technology Reports, 225 N. Michigan Ave., Suite 1300, Chicago, IL 60601-7616.

ALA TechSource
alatechsource.org

About the Author

David Lee King is the digital services director at Topeka & Shawnee County Public Library, where he plans, implements, and experiments with emerging technology trends. He speaks internationally about emerging trends, website management, digital experience, and social media and has been published in many library-related journals. David is a *Library Journal* Mover and Shaker. He has written two books: *Face2Face: Using Facebook, Twitter, and Other Social Media Tools to Create Great Customer Connections* and *Designing the Digital Experience: How to Use Experience Design Tools & Techniques to Build Websites Customers Love*. David blogs at https://davidleeking.com.

Abstract

Most of your library customers own a smartphone, using it for a variety of tasks. They want to use their smartphones in and around the library. This issue of *Library Technology Reports* (vol. 57, no. 2), "Mobile Technology in Libraries," presents tools and practices for giving your customers a great experience while connecting with your library. It addresses provisions supporting customers' mobile use inside the library, such as Wi-Fi and charging stations, or outside the building, offering mobile access for basic library tasks. The report will show ways in which libraries are using mobile technology to address the digital divide, such as circulating hot spots or training, and how staff can use mobile technology to expand services in the community.

Contents

Contents, continued

Chapter 1

The Mobile Revolution

Over the Labor Day weekend, my family visited Grinter Sunflower Farms for the first time. It's a farm in Kansas that lets people come explore the sunflower fields and take photos. It was a fun time.

We had never been there before. So, I grabbed my Canon G7X Mark II point-and-shoot camera and my iPhone and turned on Google Maps to find the farm. I followed what the app told me was the fastest route, which was accurate.

After we parked and walked to some taller sunflowers, I quickly learned that although my Canon camera takes really nice photos, the iPhone did a better job on this particular day (figure 1.1). It was still bright and sunny, and the iPhone camera has some automatic adjustments built in that change depending on what the camera sees. We ended up with some great photos.

When we returned home, my daughter and wife both AirDropped photos from my iPhone to theirs, edited the photos a bit with a photo editing app, and shared the photos to their preferred social media accounts.

See what happened? My mobile phone was an important tool that helped me enjoy the day in multiple ways—and I didn't even make a phone call! Mobile technology is now an indispensable tool for my personal life. It's also becoming indispensable to the library, as well.

The first time I saw a mobile phone was in the mid- to late 1990s. My supervisor's spouse was a Realtor, and he had a car phone. I thought it was pretty darn cool at the time.

I thought mobile phones were created sometime in the late 1980s to early 1990s; however, I was wrong. A few months ago, I was watching an *Andy Griffith Show* rerun (hey—don't knock what I binge-watch!), and someone on the show was showing off his car phone—that would be around 1966.

Out of curiosity, I did a bit of reading and found out that car phones have been around since the 1940s.

Figure 1.1
Sunflower photo taken with iPhone 11 Pro

Here's what Wikipedia said:

> In the United States, engineers from Bell Labs began work on a system to allow mobile users to place and receive telephone calls from automobiles, leading to the inauguration of mobile service on June 17, 1946 in St. Louis, Missouri. Shortly after, AT&T offered Mobile Telephone Service. A wide range of mostly incompatible mobile

telephone services offered limited coverage area and only a few available channels in urban areas. As calls were transmitted as unencrypted analog signals, they could be eavesdropped on by anyone with radio equipment that could receive those frequencies. The introduction of cellular technology, which allowed reuse of frequencies many times in small adjacent areas covered by relatively low-powered transmitters, made widespread adoption of mobile telephones economically feasible.[1]

Figure 1.2
Screenshot of Andy Griffith on a car phone

I had no idea that mobile phone technology was so old! But I do know this: the current mobile revolution has picked up a lot of steam in the last twenty years. I don't see it slowing down any time soon.

The mobile revolution as we know it today came about as a merging of mobile technologies, including mobile phones, the mobile internet, and Web 2.0. Suddenly, people had smarter devices that could connect (almost) anywhere. They could use their mobile device as a phone, and they could also capture other types of communication, such as taking photos and videos. We could suddenly type on a familiar-looking keyboard, instead of using the numeric keypad on older mobile phones. Besides text messages, we could now communicate using e-mails and through social media.

Location-based services sprang into existence, also based on mobile technology. Software programs became mobile apps downloaded from an app store. Mobile connection speeds became really important as people started to need to connect in real time to people and to an app, such as a mobile map that provides alternate routes during congestion on a highway.

And the mobile revolution was born.

Today's Mobile Technology

Today's mobile technology landscape includes lots of larger and smaller devices, connectivity to the internet, and interaction with cloud-based services. These devices include the following:

Smartphones: Smartphones, as we think of them today, have been around since Apple introduced the iPhone in 2007. The iPhone was sort of a combination of a PDA (personal digital assistant) and an easy-to-use mobile phone. Today's smartphones rely on a variety of apps for their functionality. Currently, Apple and Android devices make up the majority of the smartphone landscape.

Tablets: Tablets function much like large smartphones. They share the same operating system (OS) as a smartphone and share many apps as well. Tablets can function as a laptop replacement for some people and as a tablet-sized accessory for taking notes and for working with a variety of apps.

Laptops: Many personal computers have shrunk from desktop-based systems to more mobile-friendly laptops. You will find both Windows- and Apple-based systems.

Internet of Things: Smartphones, tablets, and laptops aren't the only mobile-friendly devices in today's mobile world. The intersection of sensors, small hardware, and cloud-based connectivity has made it easy to create small devices, connected to the internet, that do a variety of things. For example, a smartwatch or an activity monitor can count your steps, monitor your sleeping patterns, or check your heart rate.

Add-ons to mobile devices: Finally, there are add-ons to mobile devices that extend the functionality of the device. For example, you can add microphones, camera lenses, and different types of styluses (such as the Apple Pencil); cases and covers that add a keyboard to a tablet; and devices that interact with mobile apps, such as the Square credit card reader.

Square credit card reader
https://squareup.com

There's an emerging industry of smart devices that interact with the systems in your home. Think of smart light bulbs, smart window blinds, security cameras, thermostats (figure 1.3), Amazon Alexa and other smart speaker systems, or smart power outlets. Each of these home-based systems can interact with your mobile device via an app.

Apps: Apps are software programs written for a mobile device that may be purchased and downloaded from an app store. Smartphones and tablets run on app-based technology. Even your smartphone's phone is a type of mobile app. Apps also interact with the mobile device's functionality, including messaging, notifications, GPS tracking, and the mobile device's audio and camera.

Internet connection: Internet connectivity is very important in today's mobile world. You simply have to be connected to make apps and services fully function. Today's 4G standard for cell-based speeds is just starting to be replaced with faster, more stable 5G technology. The next few years should be very interesting as 5G technology becomes the new (faster) standard.

Figure 1.3
Nest Thermostat. (Source: Photo by Dan LeFebvre on Unsplash. Used with permission.)

Statistics about the Mobile Revolution

Statistics help illustrate the rapid expansion of the mobile revolution. Let's look at some numbers that show where we are in today's mobile world.

As of 2019, according to Pew Research[2]

- 81 percent of Americans own a smartphone.
- 73 percent have broadband service at home.
- 27 percent of Americans do not subscribe to home broadband.
- 37 percent of US adults say they mostly use a smartphone when accessing the internet. If you're 18 to 29 years old, that percentage goes up to 58 percent.
- 17 percent of adults are smartphone-only internet users.

To me, these statistics are pretty amazing. The first one makes sense, and I'm surprised it's not larger. I mean, if you want to own a phone these days, you are more likely to buy a cell phone rather than a landline phone. And if you purchase a cell phone, you are probably going to buy a smartphone of some type. You don't have many options when it comes to non-smart cell phones these days.

I've definitely seen the fourth statistic in action: people mostly using a smartphone to access the internet. I usually have my iPhone with me, so I'll often start a search there. If I want to do more serious exploring, I'll get my laptop. For me, using a laptop is easier when I'm opening multiple tabs, quickly scrolling around, and so on. But my twenty-year-old daughter? She has the same tools that I have, but she is definitely a smartphone-mostly internet user.

My family is very fortunate to have multiple devices and a strong Wi-Fi broadband signal in our home. Other people don't have those as an option. They might be part of the 17 percent of people who are smartphone-only internet users. If your only option is buying one device, you are most likely going to buy a smartphone. That way, you will have the ability to talk, text, e-mail, use apps, and so on. Or, more importantly, you will have a greater ability to keep in touch with family and friends.

A smartphone is not always the best device in every instance. For example, have you ever done your taxes on your phone? If so, it probably was not a stellar experience (as if doing taxes is *ever* a stellar experience). Training classes are generally better on a larger screen. Keystroking longer documents (such as this issue of *Library Technology Reports*) is much easier using a normal keyboard and more than two fingers.

Other interesting statistics on smartphone usage (from Leftronic):[3]

- Smartphone usage statistics suggest that an average person spends 2 hours and 51 minutes per day on their mobile device. What's more, 22 percent of us check our phones every few minutes, and 51 percent of users look at it a few times per hour.
- An average smartphone user has 63 interactions with a smartphone every day.
- Mobile phone usage statistics say that 90 percent of mobile time is spent on apps.
- 79 percent of adults have their smartphones with them 22 hours a day.

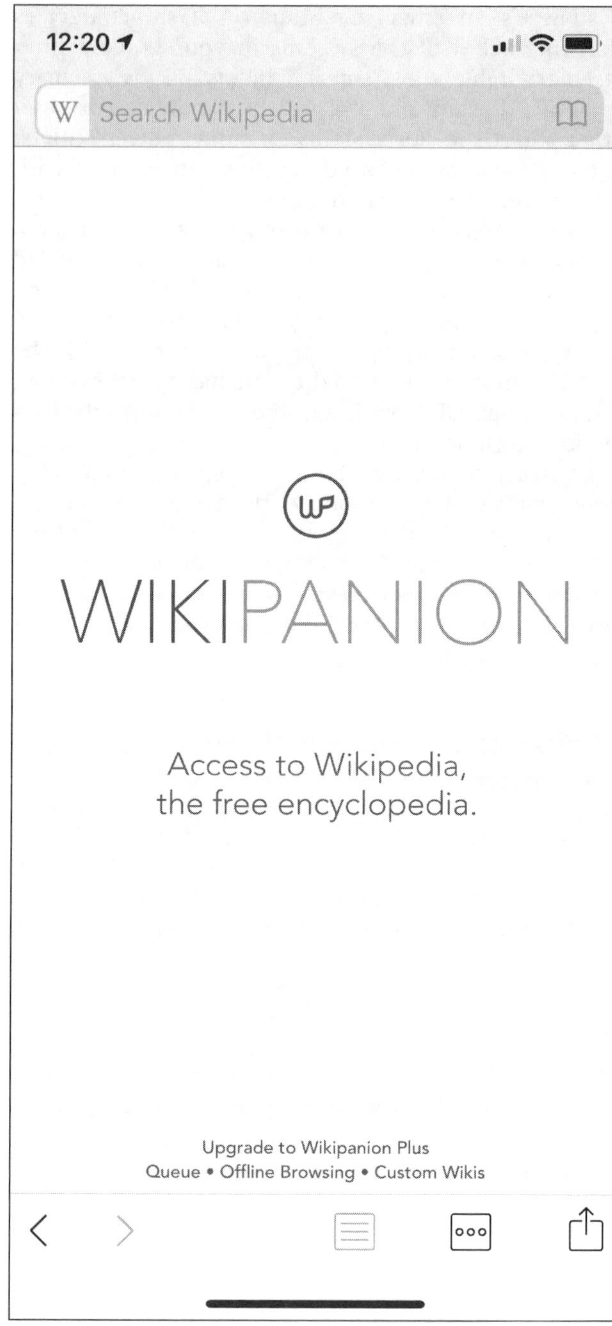

Figure 1.4
Wikipanion smartphone app

iPhones now have the ability to track usage, so I can check my own smartphone use. You can usually find this information in your smartphone settings. I fall right below the average: 2 hours, 28 minutes is my current daily average for my own smartphone use.

One other thing to note: the statistic showing that 90 percent of mobile time is spent on mobile apps is a bit misleading, I think. I've heard people quote similar stats and then say, "So we need an app for our library." I won't argue whether or not you need an app; having multiple ways to access your library is never a bad thing!

But the thing to remember with a smartphone is that every single interaction you do on a smartphone is done on an app. For that matter, the actual phone-calling part of your smartphone is performed using an app.

Plus, people do so many different things using their smartphones. For example, looking at my use, here's what you will see:

- *Social media apps* (currently TikTok, Facebook, and Instagram)—This makes sense. Social media has a mobile-first strategy that even extends to the smartphone's functionality when using those apps, like the camera, the keyboard, or even sharing your location with friends.
- *Exercise app*—I have a goal to run a 5K and am using the Couch to 5K app to track progress. This app tells me what to do when training (run, walk, etc.), keeps track of my progress, and maps my run via GPS.
- *Web browser*—I use the web browser a lot to look up random things. Safari (and Chrome, and Firefox, and Brave, etc.) are all smartphone app versions of web browsers.
- *Messaging*—I have a *lot* of different messaging services on my phone—all app-based.
- *Wikipanion*—I love this app version of Wikipedia (figure 1.4) and use it almost every day.
- *1Password*—This is a handy app that stores passwords.

I also have a variety of e-book readers, guitar tuners, metronomes, a game or two, musical instruments, to-do lists, the daily news, and so on all in app form on my phone. I turn the air conditioning on in my house with an app.

My point? Apps haven't replaced websites. Apps have replaced so much more, including physical items (e.g., a guitar tuner), utilities, print books, still and video cameras, the Franklin Planner (not that I ever actually used one of those), and even a notebook for taking notes.

This is a huge shift in our society, and it's something that librarians should try to understand about today's world (and our customers). I love what Scott Edmonds says on the Salesforce.com blog about what consumers are doing on their smartphones:

> What are they doing in those apps? Lots of stuff. According to Google, the number one smartphone activity outside of work is shopping. According to a Deloitte survey, 57 percent get their news on apps, 45 listen to music, and 31 percent stream films. Twenty-nine percent use their phones as digital

wallets, even when purchasing in-store. Many use them as smart assistants, and a growing number use them to hail transportation.[4]

How Mobile Technology Has Changed Business Practices

This leads us to our next point: how has mobile technology changed current business practices? Let's briefly examine two business practices: communication channels and equipment.

Communication Channels

Meetings in today's world don't have to be face-to-face anymore. Instead, we can use a meeting tool like Zoom or Microsoft Teams. Follow-up communications can be anything from a phone call to an e-mail to a text message.

At my library, we are currently holding all-staff meetings using Zoom. Staff connect using a variety of devices, including different types of mobile devices. They work great for this.

Equipment

Businesses install a wide variety of business-related equipment. Mobile technology has made some of this more within reach for a small business owner. It also levels the playing field for some. Here are some examples:

- *Airport ticketing.* With my smartphone, I can check in from anywhere—no more long check-in lines at the airport. Also, I have my ticket on my phone, so I don't have to juggle as many things. If the gate changes, I get a text. In this case, using app-based tools instead of traditional airport ticketing has made my life easier.
- *Credit card readers,* such as Square, have leveled the playing field for small businesses. For example, when my son was in high school, the hair stylist he went to couldn't take credit cards—just cash and checks. Then one day, she started using Square, and suddenly she could take credit card payments (which was great, because we don't usually carry cash). She didn't have to purchase a point-of-sale system. Instead, she was able to start using the Square magstripe reader and app for free.

Square
https://squareup.com

- *Social media* = more communication and connections. Obviously, social media has opened up the door for direct connections and communications to customers. It has also created new immediate customer service and support lines where they didn't necessarily exist before.
- *GPS mapping.* GPS mapping has created new businesses. For example, Uber is a business based on GPS mapping. Today, many pickup and delivery companies use GPS mapping and tracking to get around town and to find you.
- *App-based systems.* Sales reps and field operators can now track their day and daily expenses on apps and have those expenses connect back to the accounting system.
- *Visual tools.* Still and video cameras make it easier to do a variety of business-related tasks. Video conference calls definitely fall into this category. Recently, Amazon has started using smartphone cameras at delivery points. The delivery person takes a photo of your package so you know where it is (and Amazon can verify they delivered it). Personally, I've used my camera in a server room to share photos of the switch I was about to flip (to make sure it was the right one).

There are many more examples like this. Mobile technology has definitely had a major impact on business practices. The same types of changes have also affected libraries (which we'll examine in the rest of this publication).

Mobile First and Digital First

There are two terms that should be introduced before we go further: *mobile first* and *digital first.*

Mobile first design is a simple concept. It's basically what it sounds like: design for mobile devices comes first. As mobile device use increased, web-based companies (think Google and Facebook) started focusing on making sure they focused first on their mobile users.

In the library world, this means that as you redesign a website, you should focus first on the mobile experience and then design from that to larger screens. Doing this ensures that you have designed what is quickly becoming the most important user experience (the mobile one) first.

Digital first is related to having a mobile-first strategy. Having a mobile-first strategy means that you have already shifted to a digital-first strategy as well.

Here's a simple definition of digital first: "Simply put, digital-first means approaching any new opportunity, or problem, with the assumption that the solution should be *as digital as possible.*"[5]

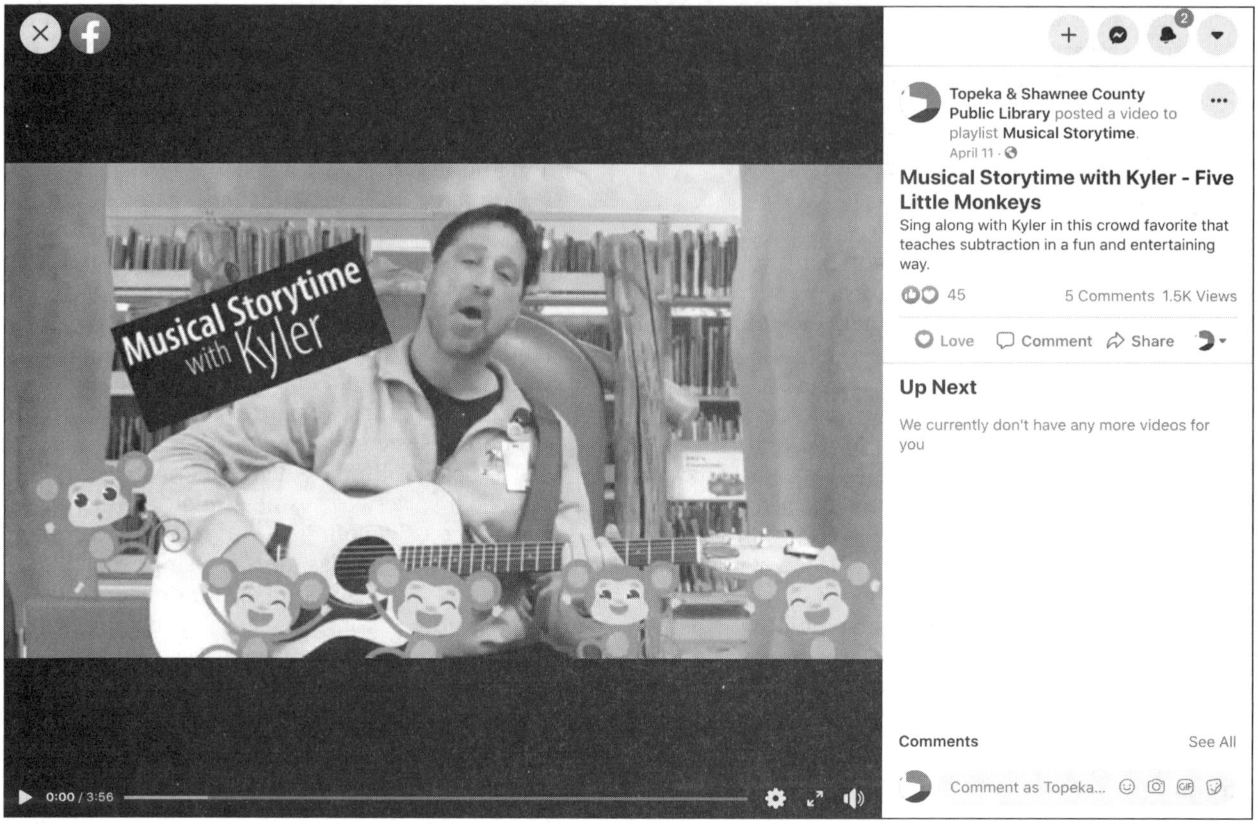

Figure 1.5
Musical Storytime with Kyler

I love that the author started out with "simply put." Because shifting to a digital-first mindset for your organization can be anything but simple. For example, a library having a digital-first mindset means to shift from primarily offering in-building services to having digital services be the primary version of that service—so storytimes, classes, events? Digital first. Calendar of events? Digital first. Here are harder ones: collections, reference questions. Yes, shift those to digital first as well.

Why move to digital first for most, if not all, library services? Moving to digital first gives more people the opportunity to use library services. For example, with a library storytime event, you can fit only so many people into a room in a library. But if you move all your storytimes online, more people can attend. You have the potential to have more people attend when the digital event happens. Your event can also be attended after the fact because it's been posted online (e.g., to your website or to YouTube).

For example, Topeka & Shawnee County Public Library is doing online only storytimes right now. One example of is this Facebook video: "Musical Storytime with Kyler—Five Little Monkeys." This storytime video (figure 1.5) has been viewed over 1,500 times on Facebook. Our largest physical space in the library building holds approximately 300 people; Kyler's storytime sessions are usually popular and draw twenty to thirty kids and parents. Having over 1,500 people virtually attend a storytime by watching a video can easily translate to one of the library's most popular events ever. Since it's in video format, it can continue to be watched until we decide to delete the video.

Global Pandemics (Hopefully *Not* Plural)

I also wanted to mention that during the current global pandemic, mobile technology has made working from home and connecting to other staff so much easier! At my library, we started working from home in March. We are mostly back to the building now, but we also have the ability to work from home as needed.

Because of the different types of mobile and digital technology tools that our staff have access to, the following have been possible:

- We have been able to send some staff home with laptops (and in some cases Wi-Fi hot spots) so they could still do their work.

- Staff are making storytime videos using their smartphones.
- Most of our back-end systems are web-based, so payroll and purchasing could easily continue from anywhere.
- E-mail and Zoom meetings were easy to set up and attend.
- File access and storage were easy because of Microsoft Office 365. We can access our work files from anywhere.

These types of things would have been *much* harder to deal with in a more traditional, non-web-based, non-mobile-technology landscape. But because we were (mostly) set up to work from anywhere, making that leap (largely over a weekend) was a relatively easy shift for us.

Emerging Trends with Mobile Technology

In case you haven't noticed, mobile technology is not slowing down. In fact, I'd say the mobile revolution is just picking up steam! For example, think about the Internet of Things and smart devices. These are largely tools and services that run on web-based and mobile apps.

Smart light bulbs, power outlets, and window shades can be controlled by an app on a phone. Many people's jobs depend on apps (delivery drivers, salespeople, Uber drivers, package delivery, etc.).

And 5G technology is right around the corner. We will continue to see mobile developments as 5G technology solidifies in the next three to five years.

How Mobile Technology Is Affecting Today's Library

This is a very exciting time. Mobile technology is changing everything about modern life, and it will also affect the library world. In fact, mobile technology is already changing how libraries operate. For example, here are some mobile-focused things that my library does:

- We have a mobile app for our website/catalog, as well as apps for databases, e-books, and mobile printing.
- Our responsive website works on mobile devices.
- Smartphones have replaced many of our service phones, desk phones, and security and maintenance phones and radios.
- RFID-enabled smart wands are used to find lost items and for inventory. This is one of many library-related tools that is built to be mobile rather than tethered to a workstation.
- My library uses tablets for our book bike service, for signing patrons up for events, as a catalog kiosk in the building, for meeting room digital signage, for study room reservations, and for creating videos.
- We are going through a Wi-Fi upgrade project this year in order to continue to offer great Wi-Fi in our building.
- Library staff can now access their files anywhere there's an internet connection using Microsoft 365.
- We currently use a mix of Zoom and Microsoft Teams for video meetings.
- We have started to move library staff from desktop workstations to a more flexible laptop-based system. This gives staff the ability to take their work laptop out of the building as needed.

And that's just scratching the surface! It's time now to take an in-depth look at mobile in the library.

Notes

1. Wikipedia, s.v. "History of Mobile Phones," last updated September 25, 2020, https://en.wikipedia.org/wiki/History_of_mobile_phones.
2. Monica Anderson, "Mobile Technology and Home Broadband 2019," Internet and Technology, Pew Research Center, June 13, 2019, https://www.pewresearch.org/internet/2019/06/13/mobile-technology-and-home-broadband-2019.
3. Marko Milijic, "29+ Smartphone Usage Statistics: Around the World in 2020," Leftronic, October 7, 2019, https://leftronic.com/smartphone-usage-statistics.
4. Scott Edmonds, "What Are Consumers Doing on Their Smartphones, Anyway?" *The 360 Blog*, Salesforce, February 26, 2018, https://www.salesforce.com/blog/consumer-smartphone-use-blog/.
5. Wilson Fletcher, "Digital-First: The Essential Modern Business Mindset," Medium, October 23, 2018, https://medium.com/thehumanlayer/digital-first-the-essential-modern-business-mindset-9e116f61407e.

Chapter 2

Mobile in the Library

Today's library patrons most likely have smartphones. In your building, someone will use their phone to look up a library book to get the call number on their smartphone's screen instead of writing it on a scrap of paper.

Another patron might send a text message while looking for a DVD for their kid's birthday party: "Do we want *Toy Story 4* or *SpongeBob*?"

Your patrons could be doing any number of things on their smartphones. How should the library interact with a person who is in your building but who is also mobile-focused? This chapter will cover how patron use of mobile technology has changed; some basic mobile technology needs—including adequate power, Wi-Fi, and comfortable furniture; ways to help patrons charge their devices; and ways to promote mobile services in the building. I will also share some fun ways to connect patrons to mobile promotions, including social media connections and hashtag signs.

Figure 2.1
Using your smartphone inside the library

Patron Use of Mobile Technology in the Library Has Changed

As more library patrons enter the library building with their phone in hand, libraries need to alter our approach for connecting with and helping these mobile device users. That's a big shift.

Some libraries have been pretty draconian about phone use in the library, even asking patrons to turn their phones off when in the library. For the most part, the people using their mobile devices weren't actually talking; they were texting (which is pretty quiet). Nonetheless, those patrons would be asked to put their phones away.

Some people will also, while looking for a book (figure 2.1), take a photo of other books they might be interested in reading. Then they will look up a book review of the book to see if it's something they want to check out. I've certainly done this in libraries, and I've also done it in bookstores.

That type of mobile phone use—texting, not talking—is a huge shift from the cell phones of old to today's multifaceted smartphones. In today's mobile-focused world, you don't usually talk to people using your phone (though it's certainly an option). Instead, you type—with a text message or a Facebook Message. If you want to share with a larger group of people, you might do that using a social media post. If you decide to talk, you might also be videoconferencing, so you can see the person while you talk.

Or if you're talking, you might not be talking to an actual person. You might be talking to a virtual assistant, such as Apple Siri, Amazon Alexa, or Google Assistant.

But your library isn't like that, you say. Your library is a phone-friendly library. That's great! So, how's your Wi-Fi signal? If you have bad Wi-Fi access in your library building, I'm not sure I'd say your building is a phone-friendly one. And that might not be your fault—many libraries aren't new buildings. Some older library buildings were built with thick walls, basements, and other things that can easily interfere with a cell phone signal.

Here's my point—a mobile device is an important tool for our patrons to have, even inside the library building. Because of this, our responsibility is to help our patrons be able to comfortably use their favorite mobile devices while they are visiting the library. We want that customer mobile experience to be a good one, whether it's outside or inside the library.

Basic Mobile Technology Needs in the Library

Hopefully, it's pretty obvious at this point that your customers will bring their mobile devices into the building with them. They might even use those devices to enhance their experience at the library.

What are you doing to help the mobile-focused part of a customer's library visit be a positive one? Here are some things to think about and improve for your mobile-focused customers.

Mobile Basics

There are some things that you can and should provide that I would call mobile basics. These are things that all mobile users will need—both experienced and novice users.

These mobile basics include the following:

- power
- great Wi-Fi
- comfortable seating options

Power: Your customers will probably need to charge their devices, especially if they use them a lot. Make sure to provide multiple ways for customers to charge their mobile devices at the point of need. More on this in a second.

Great Wi-Fi: I've already mentioned Wi-Fi a couple of times. But it's important, so I'll mention it again! Most likely, the normal cell phone signal won't be that great. Thankfully, you can provide a good Wi-Fi internet signal that will provide connectivity inside the building.

That Wi-Fi signal should be fast—24mb at a bare minimum; faster is better! It should be fast enough to do all the normal web and mobile app activities with no issues (e.g., Facebook, YouTube, games, etc.).

You should also have a robust signal that does not slow down with a lot of simultaneous use. For example, some libraries' internet still slows down in the afternoons when the kids get out of school and descend on the library. If that's the case, there's a simple solution. You need to budget for better bandwidth. I know—that costs money that you might not have. However, this is important in today's mobile-focused society. So if possible, work on setting aside money, forgo another project, or work toward being able to budget for an upgrade to your in-house Wi-Fi service.

If you need to convince a higher-up that an upgrade is needed, start by gathering information such as increased usage stats, the number of people in the building, cell phone connectivity issues, customer stories, and customer complaints. Use that information to help build an argument for updated internet.

Comfortable seating options: Have you ever needed to sit for a long time, doing something on a laptop or a phone? Most likely you have. Did you ever have to do it in an uncomfortable chair? Probably so.

Guess what? Those old, solid, dependable oak chairs that your library has had forever are not always all that comfortable to sit on for long periods of time.

But in today's mobile-focused world, we want to offer people the option to hang out at the library if they want to. These people might want to use the library's Wi-Fi to run their startup business or to write that paper for school—or just level up in their favorite game. All of these activities are things that a library patron might find important to do while they are visiting the library.

This is easy to fix. Start researching more comfortable seating options and arrangements. There are some modern comfortable seating options with flip-up tables and USB plug options, which is great.

If people want to hang out together, make sure this furniture is movable! An impromptu study group or group project is so much easier when you can work (and sit, and power up) together.

Helping Customers Recharge

Adequate and easy-to-access power is also important in today's mobile-focused world. A few years ago, I discovered that my library did not have adequate power options for customers. I was walking around the building and noticed something interesting. At the time, we had these little wooden tables with lamps

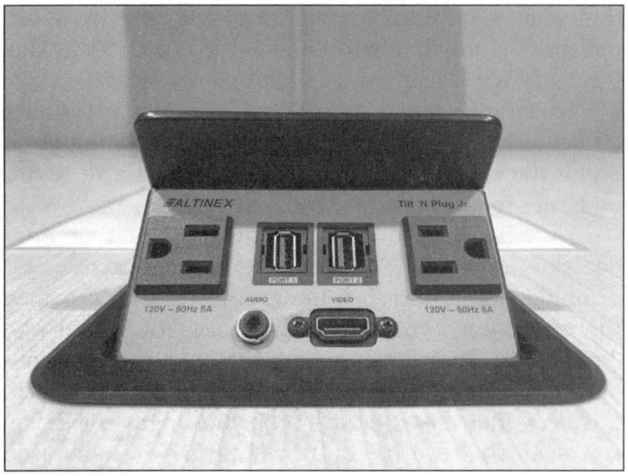

Figure 2.2
USB outlet installed on a table

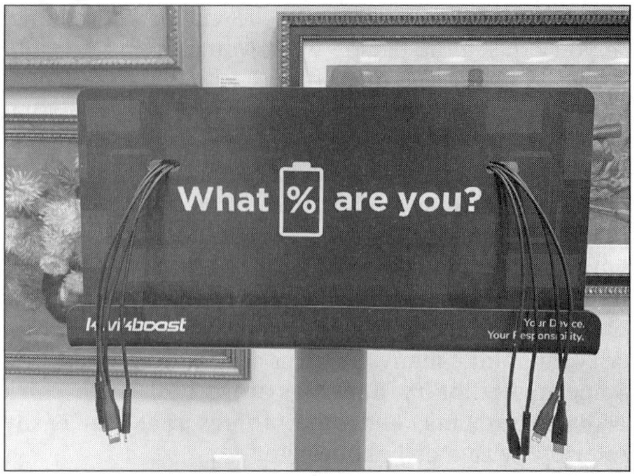

Figure 2.3
Charging station at the library

attached to the table. The lamps were supposed to be plugged into the wall.

Guess what? Almost all of the lamps were unplugged. Why? Because people with mobile devices were sitting in the chairs by the tables. They needed to recharge their devices, so they unplugged the lamps and plugged in their devices. And then forgot to plug the lamps back in when they were done.

Thankfully, there are easy ways to offer power and charging stations in the library. For starters, your library probably has a variety of normal electrical outlets throughout the building. If that's all you have—great! Don't block them. Rearrange library furniture so power outlets are easy to access.

If you have tables pushed up against the walls and there are power outlets under the tables, simply attach a power bar under the table (you might have seen this at some airports). That way, anyone sitting at or around the tables will be able to charge up their devices without having to wiggle themselves under the table to reach the power outlets.

My library retrofitted some of our older tables with pop-up power and USB outlets (figure 2.2). So instead of just having a table, we now have tables with a couple of power outlets in the middle of the table.

You can go one step further than easy access to power outlets and can set up mobile charging stations. There are many different types of charging stations. My library has two types. We have a couple of those charging stations on a stand (figure 2.3). They offer different mobile device cables. That works great in a shared space or an area where people might gather. We have placed those in our teen room, in a common seating area, and by a comfortable seating area in the Kids Library, by our aquarium. There are toddler toys in that part of the building, and parents and kids like to hang out in that space. The parents talk, the kids play, and their devices get recharged.

Figure 2.4
Power outlet pole

We also have a power outlet charging station. It's basically a short pole that stands upright with six power outlets on it (figure 2.4). We have it by a table. I've seen these deployed in a library's common seating or gathering area and thought it was a fabulous idea. Often people have power adapters with them—so they might not need a mobile phone cable, but just easy access to a power outlet.

Some libraries offer portable battery chargers that can be checked out at a service desk. One step up from that is Temple University's Battery Share service. Here's what Temple says about its Battery Share service:

> Temple Center City now has a kiosk containing 24 portable battery units called power banks for charging your laptop or mobile devices. As a student, you can borrow a power bank and bring it to your classroom. After class, you can then return the power bank to the kiosk. This service is free, and the borrowing period is up to five hours, depending on when the building closes. Note: Each power bank includes a standard three-prong outlet and USB ports, but does not include the cables that connect to your devices. So you make sure to please bring your own.[1]

Make sure that your customers can use their mobile devices in your building. Also make sure that they can leave the library 100 percent powered up!

Promoting Mobile Services in the Building

You have decided that patrons are welcome to use smartphones in the building. You have purchased comfortable seating, and you have great Wi-Fi. Now, how can you promote your mobile offerings to your mobile-focused library customers? There are many ways to do this. Here are some places to start.

Signs: Start by simply hanging signs on the walls! Use simple signage to point customers to your digital services, and place these signs and posters in strategic places. For example, if your library has an audiobook collection, place signs for Hoopla's and OverDrive's digital audiobook collections close to the physical audiobooks. Do the same thing with Hoopla and DVD videos.

You could add some signs pointing to OverDrive by the mystery collection and add some signage about Freegal close to the music CD collection. Adding signs that point to your digital collections can help promote these digital collections to patrons who are already using the physical versions of the collection.

Think about the signs you see in a department store and consider similar signage. Have you seen signs that say something like "More items can be found at mystore.com"? These signs are a good reminder that more colors and sizes are offered online.

A library can use the same strategy. At any given time, a large part of your collection is checked out. Remind people that they don't have to visit that same shelf five times to get the next book in a series. Instead, they can just go to your website and put the book on hold. This is important because the only way to access your library's full collection is online.

Figure 2.5
QR code on a sign at the library

QR codes: QR codes are coming back into vogue, and this time around they are easier to use. Modern smartphone camera apps automatically read a QR code and direct the user to a website for more information, so no secondary app is needed.

My library is using QR codes on signs in the building (figure 2.5), so you can quickly find more information about some of our new services, such as our new curbside pickup service. Just aim your phone at the QR code, and you are immediately presented with the page pointing to information about the library service.

Because of the current COVID-19 pandemic, we have mobile-focused signs outside the building as well. Our Wi-Fi signal stretches outside the building and is accessible from 7 a.m. to 10 p.m. every day. We communicate this to our customers via a sign (figure 2.6). We also share where to park in order to access the strongest signal. That way, people can easily socially distance in our parking lot and connect to the things they need through a strong Wi-Fi signal provided by the library.

Library staff is an important part of these newer mobile-focused services. If your staff doesn't know how to connect to Wi-Fi on different types of devices or how to download and use a mobile app for your library's digital content, they won't be able to provide good customer service to your library patrons.

It's relatively easy to help your staff learn mobile-focused services through staff training initiatives. Make sure to train your library's staff on everything that you offer to your mobile customers. Buy a smartphone or two if needed. Train staff on the basics of different mobile OSs (operating systems), show them how to download mobile apps (and what app stores to use) and how to connect different types of devices to your library's Wi-Fi system.

While you're at it, go one step further with staff and teach them how to gently "upsell" the library. According to Wikipedia:

> Upselling is a sales technique where a seller invites the customer to purchase more expensive items, upgrades, or other add-ons to generate more revenue. While it usually involves marketing more profitable services or products, it can be simply exposing the customer to other options that were perhaps not considered (A different technique is cross-selling in which a seller tries to sell something else). In practice, large businesses usually combine upselling and cross-selling to maximize revenue.[2]

Obviously, in a library we're not trying to sell a customer more expensive products. But we can do a type of upselling by simply sharing other similar services with our customers. For example, when customers check items out at the circulation desk, circulation staff can "upsell" by letting customers know about the library's new mobile app for catalog access and showing them how to download the app. Or when librarians help customers find books on the shelf, they can share information about the Libby e-book mobile app.

Upselling is a simple tweak to a library's customer service that can add a lot of mobile traffic through simple conversations about a library's digital services. If staff members have a smartphone or tablet with them, they can even show the customer where to download the app and demonstrate how it works.

Mobile Promotions in the Building

We can have a lot of fun with customers in the building if they have their mobile devices with them by offering selfie-focused promotions that use a mobile phone camera, hashtags, and social media. Here are some examples.

Selfie Stations

Set up some creative selfie stations in your building. My library has set up an iPad with a selfie station app

Figure 2.6
Best Wi-Fi sign in the library's parking lot

on a stand, usually connected to an event at the library (such as summer reading). We'll have fun backdrops people can use and accessories to hold for the photo. The app we use has different filters and backgrounds, so it makes it fun to take a picture of yourself and your friends. After taking the photo, patrons can share the photo via e-mail or text message. From there, they can share the photo on social media.

If you don't have a selfie station, you can skip that part and simply set up a fun backdrop and provide props. Then direct people to take photos and share them to social media.

Hashtags for Library Selfies

When you use selfie stations, make sure to have signs directing customers to use a specific hashtag when they post their photos to social media. In this way, when someone posts their photo to Instagram or Facebook, everyone will be able to see the photo by clicking on the hashtag. It's a fun, free way to get some customer-created library promotion of an event.

The city of Topeka, Kansas (where I live), has gone a step further with hashtags. A local nonprofit organization, Greater Topeka Partnership, has created a large physical version of a hashtag (#topcity) that it carts around the city. People take photos of themselves and others with the hashtag and share it. It's a way to promote living in Topeka.

Your library might also have what I call "Instagram-able areas" of the library. In my library, we have a few Instagram-able areas: our aquarium is one. You can get a selfie with a fish! Our Kids Library is pretty cool, with large murals, boats to sit in, and even some dinosaur legs (yes, we have dinosaur legs). Put some hashtag signs up by these areas in the library. Encourage people to snap photos of themselves and their kids and share them to social media.

Hashtags and selfies in the library are great ways to help patrons share the fun of visiting the library. As an added bonus, you can (with permission) re-share those photos and videos on your library's social media channels. It's a great way to capture authentic use of your library building, which people love seeing.

Notes

1. "Battery Share," Temple University Information Technology Services, accessed September 9, 2020, https://its.temple.edu/battery-share.
2. Wikipedia, s.v. "Upselling," last updated August 18, 2020, https://en.wikipedia.org/wiki/Upselling.

Chapter 3

Mobile outside the Library

The last chapter provided some ideas for helping a library's mobile-focused customers when they are visiting the library—but what about when they leave the building? For the most part, your library customers are at home, at work, or at school. Even your regular customers spend most of their time outside the library.

Thankfully, we have the capability to use mobile technology to connect with those customers. If they have a smartphone and a couple of apps, they can still use the library, even if they are not in your building.

This chapter covers the mobile technology needs that your customers might have when they are away from the library, including checking out materials, reading library news, receiving library-focused notifications, accessing e-books and other e-resources, and asking questions.

This chapter also covers mobile access to the library's website, the library catalog, and databases; mobile apps the library has; and ways a library can connect with customers using a mobile device (including social media and podcasts). I'll also discuss other opportunities to use mobile technology in the community (for example, with area schools).

Basic Library Activities Using Mobile Technology

The majority of your customers have the capability to do quite a few library-related tasks using a mobile device. For example, if customers have smartphones, they should be able to visit your website, browse the library catalog, and use a database. If those websites are not mobile-friendly, it might not be the greatest experience in the world, but they can at least access the website.

Let's explore some basic library activities that can be done using a mobile device, including

- checking out materials
- accessing e-books and other e-resources
- reading library news
- getting notifications
- asking a question

Checking Out Materials

Checking out materials is foundational to libraries. Most libraries have, at this point, moved their library catalogs (integrated library systems, or ILSs) to an online system, where customers can search, find items, put books on hold, and take care of account-related tasks such as updating a phone number.

Your customers should also be able to perform these basic library tasks from a mobile device. There are a couple of ways this can be accomplished. Today, most ILSs can be accessed using a mobile web browser; however, the user experience will vary greatly. Some ILSs have created a responsive, mobile-friendly version that works well on mobile web browsers. Other systems are not there yet. In some cases, customers can navigate to the catalog, but they will then need to pinch and zoom to make the website readable.

Another way to accomplish using the catalog on a mobile device is to access it through a mobile app. Some ILSs have a mobile app version of the catalog. If they do not offer this feature, there are third-party mobile apps that include this type of functionality. My library, for example, uses a mobile app that we purchased from Communico (figure 3.1).[1]

A third option to make an ILS work in a mobile setting is to install a discovery overlay that sits on top of the ILS. A discovery overlay is a way to provide extended functionality and features to an existing ILS's customer-facing library catalog. BiblioCommons is a great example of a discovery overlay that uses responsive web design. It easily adapts to any number of mobile devices.

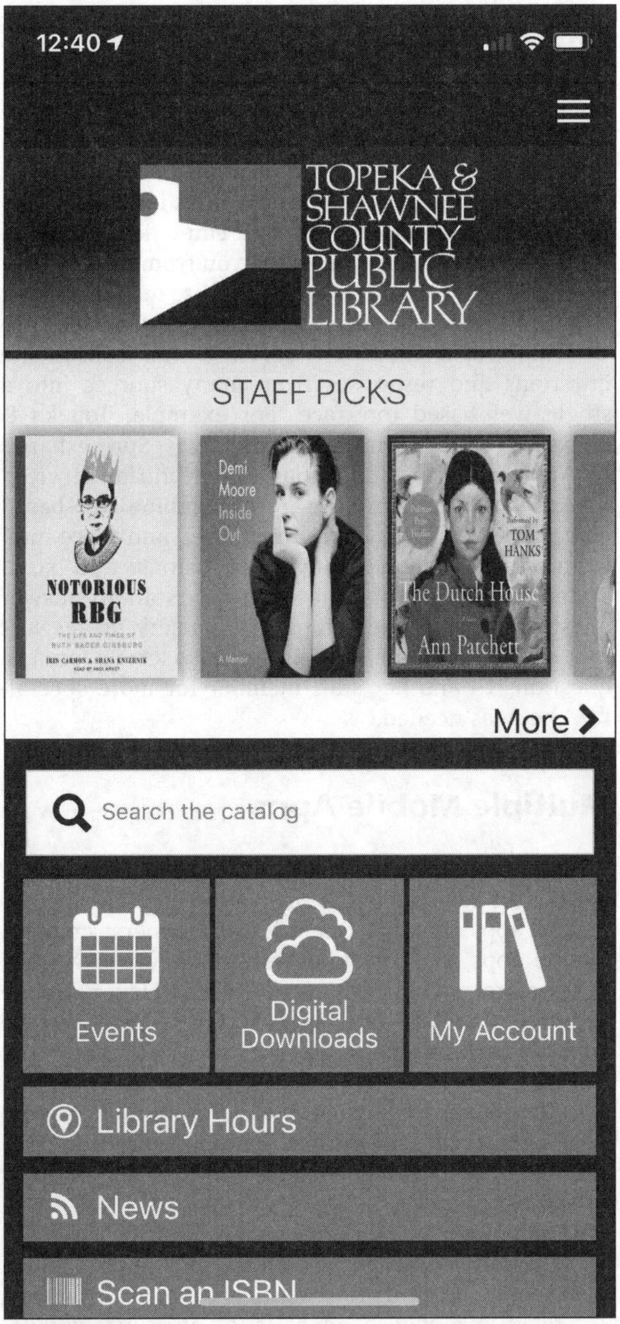

Figure 3.1
Topeka & Shawnee County Public Library's mobile app from Communico

Accessing E-books and Other E-resources

Today's library has a large collection of e-collections. Often, a library doesn't include e-books, streaming video, and other online resources as part of its total collection count, but it should. A library can spend a large percent of its collection budget on e-resources; it makes sense to treat these resources the same way we treat other resources in the library.

To maximize the impact of e-collections, we need to help library customers access a library's e-content in an easy way. Sometimes there is a simple solution. For example, if you use OverDrive for e-books, all you have to do is point customers to the mobile app and help them connect to the library's e-book collection. After that, the customer has instant access to the collection.

The tricky part is figuring out the best way to share that your library has e-content in the first place. We have all heard a library customer say something like, "I didn't know the library had e-books!" Our customers don't know because the library hasn't done a great job of promoting the service.

Sometimes, even finding information about the service—let alone finding a link to the mobile app—can be challenging. Now multiply those challenges by all the e-resources your library has. For example, Topeka & Shawnee County Public Library has eighty-five databases and eleven mobile apps. It is definitely a challenge to promote all of our e-content along with everything else the library does.

Reading Library News

People want to know what's happening at the library. They might be interested in major events at the library, or they might be interested in finding out more about a new library service.

Can library news be delivered to library customers in a mobile format? Yes, it can—through responsive-designed websites with a news section, through electronic newsletters, and through social media channels.

There are also different ways to "subscribe" to library news. RSS feeds and RSS feed readers are still simple and useful tools for getting updated content from a website. RSS functionality is included in many modern websites.

Electronic newsletters are also an easy way to share library news and updates. You can set up a newsletter through many services, including Mailchimp, Constant Contact, or OrangeBoy. Customers sign up for the newsletter using an e-mail address, so news of the library is delivered to their e-mail inbox.

Make sure you use multiple ways to share library news so your customers know what's happening at the library.

Getting Notifications

Here is a good explanation of notifications from Airship.com:

> A push notification is a message that pops up on a mobile device. App publishers can send them at any time; users don't have to be in the app or using their devices to receive them. They can do a lot of things; for example, they can show the latest sports scores, get a user to take an action, such as downloading a coupon, or let a user know about an event, such as a flash sale. Push notifications look like SMS text messages and mobile alerts, but they only reach users who have installed your app. Each mobile platform has support for push notifications—iOS, Android, Fire OS, Windows and BlackBerry all have their own services.[2]

In the library world, a notification might be a Facebook Live post to communicate something to customers, for example. When my library "goes live" on Facebook, the Facebook app sends a notification to everyone who follows the library on Facebook, letting them know that the library is sharing a live video. Then, if people seeing the notification click on it, the app will open, and they can watch the live video.

There are some library-focused mobile app companies that are creating this type of functionality in their mobile apps. For example, Capira Technologies (now part of OCLC) builds mobile apps for libraries that send push notifications. Here's what Capira Technologies says about the types of notifications its app can send to customers who have downloaded the mobile app:

> Push Notifications are also a great way to highlight your library's events and promotions. Do you have a program that isn't getting the number [of] registrations you want? Send out a Push Notification with a link directly to the registration page for that program, and watch your numbers increase right away. Promoting your Facebook page with a raffle or some other contest for those who "like" your page? Deploy a Push Notification informing your users about the promotion, and watch the number of "likes" go up and up, minute by minute after deploying your message![3]

Asking a Question

One major function of a library is to answer questions. Most libraries have a traditional reference desk to help customers inside the building. In an online setting, libraries have different types of ask-a-librarian services.

A library customer who is not in the library building can simply use the phone and call the reference desk. But today's mobile library customers aren't limited to making a phone call. Depending on what types of mobile reference services a library uses, library customers can also use SMS text messaging to ask a question. They might ask a question using Facebook Messenger. They might send a question using e-mail, or they might send a DM (direct message) using Twitter. A library can also set up an ask-a-librarian service in a mobile communication app such as Telegram or WhatsApp and answer questions there.

If your library offers multiple ways for library customers to ask questions online, it can quickly get confusing with questions coming at you from phone calls, web-based chat services, voice mails, text messages, e-mail, Facebook, Twitter, Instagram, and WhatsApp!

Thankfully, there are services that consolidate questions and responses from many sources into a single web-based interface. For example, Topeka & Shawnee County Public Library uses Springshare's LibAnswers to consolidate our ask-a-librarian service.[4] LibAnswers allows my library to combine web-based chat, text messages, e-mail messages, and voice mail from our VoIP phone system into a single web-based system for staff. This allows library staff to answer questions and to keep track of a variety of answers for use at a later date. LibAnswers also lets us forward questions to another staff member for more specialized help, as needed.

Multiple Mobile Apps

I have already mentioned library-focused mobile apps, but I have one more suggestion about a library's mobile apps that are offered to customers: create a mobile apps page on your website (figure 3.2). As I said before, my library currently has eleven mobile apps for a variety of library services. Here are the apps we currently point to:

- Communico's Engage Mobile App Library App (connects to the library catalog, our event calendar, and other information on the library's website)
- Libby (one of OverDrive's e-book apps)
- OverDrive (OverDrive's first e-book app)
- Hoopla Digital (e-books, audiobooks, movies, television shows, educational and instructional videos, documentaries, and music)
- Flipster (digital magazine collection)
- SmartAlec (mobile printing service from Comprise Technologies)
- Creativebug (a craft-based app)
- Lynda (a collection of instructional videos)
- Mango Languages (a language learning app)
- EBSCOhost (access to EBSCOhost databases)
- Beanstack (We use this for reading challenges and our summer reading program.)

A library's collection of mobile apps can add up fast! So it makes sense to create a mobile apps page

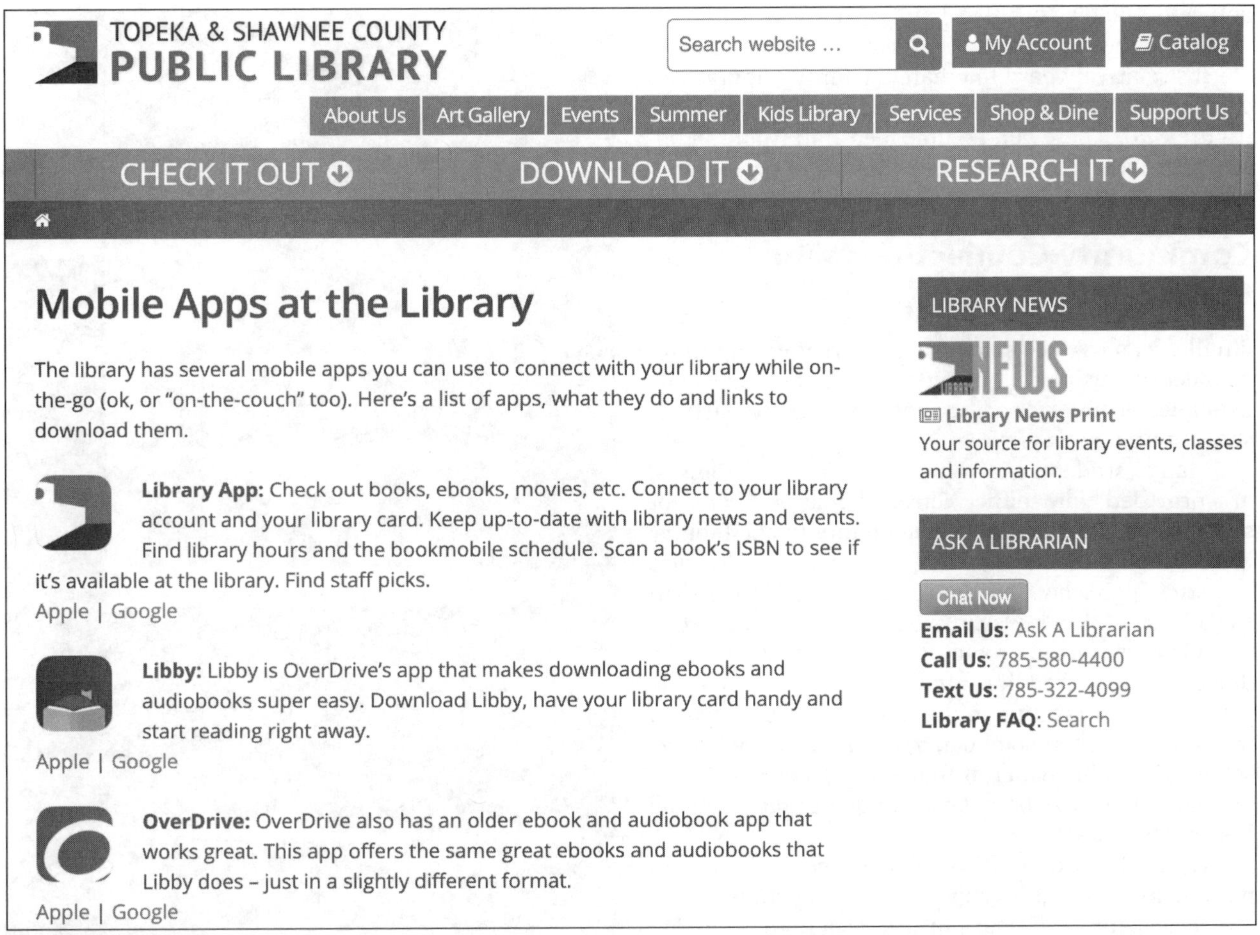

Figure 3.2
Topeka's mobile apps page

on your website. Topeka & Shawnee County Public Library's mobile apps page includes a short description of each mobile app.[5] We also provide links to the Apple and Google app stores for each app, which helps make finding and downloading all the library's mobile apps much easier for our library customers.

Social Media

One reason social media is so popular is because of mobile devices. Social media apps work great on mobile devices, and many people have at least one mobile device with them for most of the day.

This makes communicating through social media very easy! A part of a modern library's communication to customers includes creating social media posts on a variety of social media services. Most likely, your customers will have installed at least one of these social media apps. If they have followed your social media channel, they will receive updates as you post them.

What social media services should a library use? If we look at national statistics, you should definitely think about using Facebook and YouTube. In the United States, Pew Research reports that 69 percent of adults use Facebook, and 73 percent use YouTube.[6]

That means your library needs to create multimedia content. Text-based posts work fine on Facebook, but photo- and video-based content tends to get more interaction. And of course, YouTube is a video-based service.

Some of these services send notifications to a follower's mobile device when new content gets posted. For example, Facebook, Instagram, and YouTube all allow content creators to share live videos and more ephemeral, temporary content such as Stories. When someone posts these types of content, the mobile app sends a notification letting users know there's a new story or live video.

Podcasts are another type of multimedia content to consider creating. Podcasts work great on mobile devices because there are apps focused on subscribing to podcasts. For example, Apple devices have an app called Podcasts built for following podcasts from Apple's iTunes collection of podcasts.

It's relatively easy to create a twenty-minute podcast about library news or book recommendations (figure 3.3). These can be uploaded into Apple's Podcast service and then promoted to library customers.

Community Connections with Mobile Technology

Finally, let's explore some ways to create community connections using mobile technology. Here are some examples of libraries using their community partnerships in unique ways.

Many students in Shawnee County, Kansas, are provided with either Chromebooks or iPads for schoolwork. Topeka & Shawnee County Public Library has worked with local school districts to make sure the students' school-supplied tablets work well with the library's Wi-Fi systems. For some reason, when schools first started providing tablets to students, the devices were locked down in a way that restricted the tablet from connecting to the library's Wi-Fi network. My library's technology department worked with the school IT departments to figure out what was going on and how to fix the issue so students could use the library's Wi-Fi system.

We could also work with local school districts to get our library mobile apps installed on student tablets. For example, if your library has a library catalog mobile app, this would ensure that all students have easy access to your library catalog. Then, you could even set up training classes to train teachers on how to use the library's mobile apps.

Some libraries have partnered with local cultural centers and museums to create interesting partnership learning opportunities centered around a mobile app. For example, the Carroll County Public Library in Carroll County, Maryland, partnered with a local museum and a local technology company to create an augmented reality exhibit. Here's more information from its website about the exhibit:

> The Union Mills: Early Industry Comes Alive exhibit is a partnership between the Carroll County Public Library, The Union Mills Homestead, and Balti Virtual to engage the community in local history. This project combines a traveling exhibit of artifacts with augmented reality animations to offer an interactive experience. This project was funded by a Library Services and Technology Act Grant from the Institute of Museum and Library Services and the Maryland State Library. View the augmented reality animations for the grist mill and tannery using the free HoloTats app available at the App Store or Google Play. Open the HoloTats app and scan the grist mill and tannery images noted below to bring each to life. Don't forget to turn on your sound.[7]

Figure 3.3
Topeka's podcast

These are just a few ideas of ways to partner with other organizations in your community using a library's mobile apps. The opportunities are endless!

Notes

1. "Engage," Communico, accessed September 26, 2020, https://communico.us/patron-app-936.
2. "Push Notifications Explained," Airship, accessed September 26, 2020, https://www.airship.com/resources/explainer/push-notifications-explained.
3. "Push Notifications," Capira Technologies, accessed August 11, 2020, https://www.capiratech.com/push-notification.
4. "LibAnswers + Social," Springshare, https://www.springshare.com/libanswers.
5. "Mobile Apps at the Library," Topeka & Shawnee County Public Library, https://tscpl.org/mobile-apps-at-the-library.
6. Andrew Perrin and Monica Anderson, "Share of U.S. Adults Using Social Media, Including Facebook, Is Mostly Unchanged Since 2018," Pew Research Center, April 10, 2019, https://www.pewresearch.org/fact-tank/2019/04/10/share-of-u-s-adults-using-social-media-including-facebook-is-mostly-unchanged-since-2018.
7. "Union Mills: Early Industry Comes Alive," Carroll County Public Library, accessed September 26, 2020, https://library.carr.org/programs/unionmills.asp.

Chapter 4

The Digital Divide

This chapter introduces the digital divide and how it relates to mobile technology. First, I cover what the digital divide is, and then I'll discuss how libraries are helping bridge this divide by offering ways to check out equipment, partnering with local organizations and programs, and training people to better use mobile technology.

The digital divide is an important issue facing our communities. Think about your own daily technology use for a second. What do you normally do on your phone or tablet? I use everyday technology for reading, keeping up with the news, and keeping up with my checking account. I use it as a communication device: I can keep up with friends, family, and colleagues through e-mail, texting, social media, or the phone. I also use my phone as an easy-to-use reference tool. I probably look something up on Wikipedia every day, using the Wikipanion app.

I store photos, passwords, and thoughts throughout the day on my phone. I can access thousands of songs on any of my devices because everything is synced to iCloud. I use my phone for work and for fun (figure 4.1).

This level of use is probably fairly typical for many people. However, this level of use is possible only with two things: a mobile device (obviously) and a stable connection to the internet.

In contrast,

> . . . the Federal Communications Commission estimates that more than 21 million people in the United States don't have that connection [the internet]. That includes nearly 3 in 10 people—27 percent—who live in such rural places as the outreaches of Maine and the fertile fields of Indiana, as well as 2 percent of those living in cities.[1]

That quote is talking about people who do not have access to the internet. If you add in people who don't have access to "acceptable internet"—an internet signal that is fast and stable enough to do the types of activities I mentioned above—it's a much larger number:

> And those estimates are on the low side. Other research, including analysis from Microsoft, suggests that the number of Americans without broadband—that's internet access with download speeds of at least 25 megabytes per second (Mbps) and upload speeds of at least 3 Mbps—could be over 163 million.[2]

There's definitely a digital divide in the United States. Even in Shawnee County, Kansas, where I live, there's an interesting digital divide that crosses different types of boundaries. Some people in Shawnee County don't have the ability to subscribe to broadband internet services or cell phone providers because of the cost. It's available to them, but they can't afford it.

A second issue is coverage. We have urban and suburban areas in the city, and we also have rural areas in the county. There are people with large, nice homes who live in rural areas of the county who can certainly afford broadband, but it's not available to them because the service doesn't extend to those areas.

The same thing holds true with cell phone signals: sometimes, they don't reach rural areas. Travelers may lose cell phone connection while driving through rural areas on major highways between cities.

As our world quickly moves online and mobile, adequate access to the internet becomes an important issue that libraries can help tackle.

Some Definitions

When talking about the digital divide, there is some terminology we need to nail down in order to

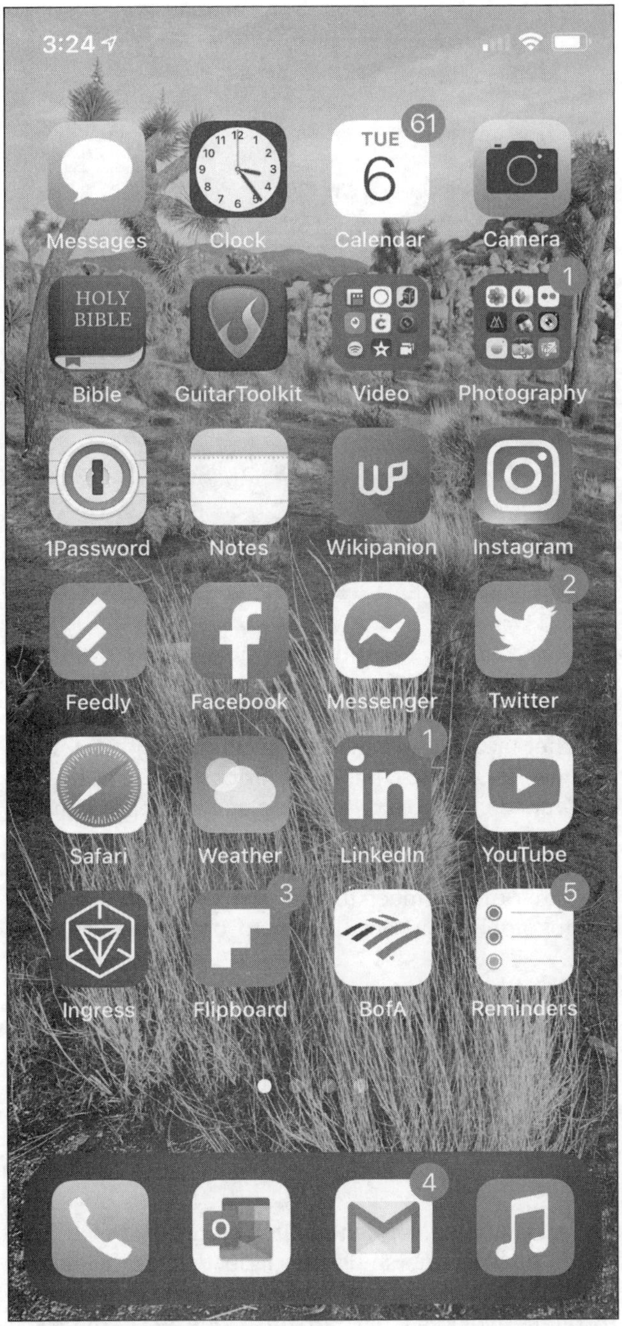

Figure 4.1
First screen of my iPhone

understand the issues involved.

- **Digital divide.** "A **digital divide** is any uneven distribution in the access to, use of, or impact of information and communications technologies (ICT) between any number of distinct groups, which can be defined based on social, geographical, or geopolitical criteria, or otherwise."[3]
- **Digital inclusion.** "Digital Inclusion refers to the activities necessary to ensure that all individuals and communities, including the most disadvantaged, have access to and use of Information and Communication Technologies (ICTs). This includes 5 elements: 1) affordable, robust broadband internet service; 2) internet-enabled devices that meet the needs of the user; 3) access to digital literacy training; 4) quality technical support; and 5) applications and online content designed to enable and encourage self-sufficiency, participation and collaboration. Digital Inclusion must evolve as technology advances. Digital Inclusion requires intentional strategies and investments to reduce and eliminate historical, institutional and structural barriers to access and use technology."[4]
- **Digital equity.** "Digital Equity is a condition in which all individuals and communities have the information technology capacity needed for full participation in our society, democracy and economy. Digital Equity is necessary for civic and cultural participation, employment, lifelong learning, and access to essential services."[5]
- **Digital literacy.** Digital literacy is "the ability to use information and communication technologies to find, evaluate, create, and communicate information, requiring both cognitive and technical skills."[6]

Many of these concepts can be folded into the umbrella term *digital inclusion* because that definition includes connectivity, devices, training, and tech support needs.

How Are Libraries Bridging the Divide?

Libraries can help bridge this digital divide through offering different types of internet access, offering ways to borrow and use technology equipment, making partnerships in the community, and offering training programs aimed at teaching internet basics.

Access to Equipment

Traditionally, libraries have helped narrow the digital divide in relation to internet access and equipment. Libraries started purchasing computers for customers to use in the 1980s and have been offering internet access since soon after the World Wide Web was created in the early 1990s.

Today's modern library generally offers up-to-date computers connected to the internet, usually with a wired network connection (figure 4.2). The library also offers public Wi-Fi access for customers who want to connect to the internet using their own devices.

Some libraries offer laptops and tablets for

customers to borrow. Mostly, this equipment can be used while in the library building. Some libraries allow customers to check out equipment to take home.

For example, Kings County Library, in the Seattle, Washington area, offers laptops for checkout.[7] A library customer can check the laptops out only within the building. Even though the service is just available in-building, it's still a very nice option to go anywhere within the building with the equipment.

Other libraries allow patrons to check out Chromebooks and other types of tablets. Some libraries offer other types of devices that can be checked out, such as microphones or music-related MIDI keyboards.

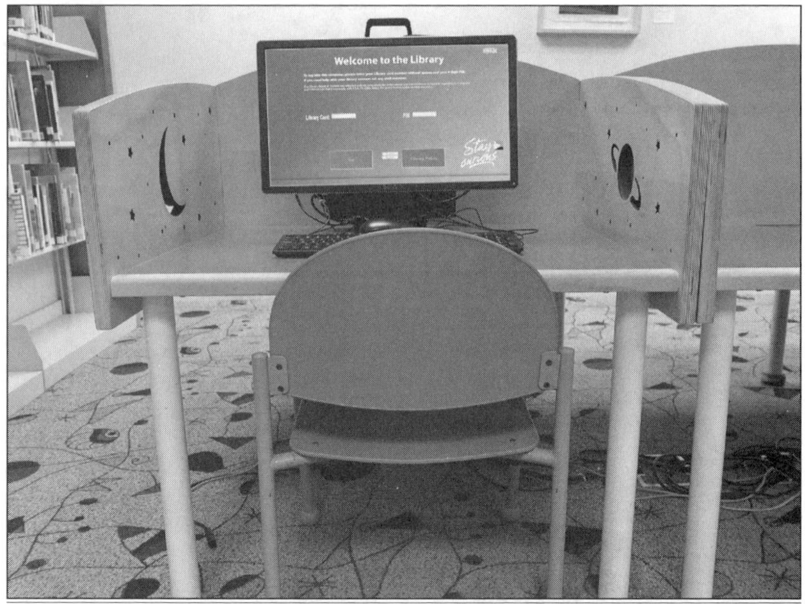

Figure 4.2
Public computer at Topeka & Shawnee County Public Library

Access to the Internet

The ability to check out and use different pieces of equipment is a great service to offer customers. But what if someone could check out the entire internet? Well, that's exactly what some libraries are doing when they allow a customer to check out Wi-Fi hot spots, which allow internet access.

For example, DeKalb County Public Library in Decatur, Georgia, offers Wi-Fi hot spots for checkout for twenty-one days.[8] Libraries that I've talked to that offer Wi-Fi hot spot checkout all report that this service is a popular one. Most say the biggest problem they have is that they don't have enough hot spots to check out. These devices always have hold requests placed on them and are in high demand.

In an article on the Google Fiber website, Jill Joplin, executive director of the DeKalb County Library Foundation, shares this information about DeKalb County Public Library's Wi-Fi hotspot service:[9]

- The library offers 200 Wi-Fi hot spots to check out.
- More than 50 percent of patrons who check out these devices do not have access to the internet in their home.
- Staff at the library realized a few years ago that patrons were accessing the library's Wi-Fi signal during times the library was closed by sitting in the parking lot or on the steps of the building.

I think it's great that this library noticed a need and responded to it by creating a service to help customers.

At Topeka & Shawnee County Public Library, we do a few things that help bridge the digital divide. For starters, we offer fast Wi-Fi and wired broadband internet access within our building, and we have around 180 public computers for customers to use.

Outside the library building, we also offer connectivity in several ways. Our bookmobiles are equipped with public Wi-Fi hot spots. This allows our library customers to connect to the internet in and around a bookmobile without having to use their own data plan.

The library also maintains eight computer labs in community centers around the county. Each of these computer labs offers Wi-Fi access and computers that can be used with a library card.

Local Partnerships That Help Bridge the Digital Divide

The community computer labs example above illustrates how partnerships can help bridge the digital divide. This particular project was accomplished through two local partnerships: one with the local county parks and recreation department, which maintains the county's community centers, and one with our local public housing authority. The housing authority maintains a community center at one of its housing areas, and we placed a computer center there and have taught technology classes at the computer lab (figure 4.3). In our case, two partnerships turned into eight computer labs and approximately fifty computers for people in Shawnee County, Kansas, to use and enjoy.

Partnerships between like-minded organizations can be a great way to get devices and internet access to people who need it the most. For example, Kansas

Figure 4.3
Community computer lab partnership

City Public Library (in Kansas City, Missouri) participates in DigitalInclusionKC. Here is its vision: "Every citizen and household in the Kansas City metropolitan area has access to the Internet, the equipment needed to use it and the skills needed to take advantage."[10] The steering council of DigitalInclusionKC includes people from the library, city government, and local nonprofits focused on digital inclusion initiatives.

Partnerships can help with more than just basic technology and connectivity needs. Some organizations help get emerging technology to library customers. For example, the California State Library has offered grants to California libraries for a variety of technology needs.[11] In the past, it has offered grants for libraries to receive virtual reality (VR) technology devices for use for library customers, a shared e-book platform, and broadband grants. Each of these grants helps an individual library, which in turn will be able to use that technology to help their local library customers.

Training Customers to Use Mobile Technology

Offering cool equipment like iPads, laptops, and gigabit internet connectivity does no good if your customers don't really know what to do with those things. That's why training is a vital aspect of bridging the digital divide.

As I stated earlier in this chapter, many libraries have traditionally offered technology training programs. Much of my own library career has been focused on training patrons and library staff to use technology: computers, mice, tablets, phones, apps, websites, software, and so on. Many libraries have built training labs, offer technology walk-in sessions, and offer other types of technology training that helps teach people how to utilize technology.

It's important for libraries to continue to offer technology training for emerging mobile technology devices. Some libraries have offered classes such as "how to use an e-book" or have given an introduction to an iPad, for example. We need to continue offering those basic classes, while also continually developing new classes around mobile technology needs. These classes might very well shift over time, as mobile technology continues to evolve.

For example, libraries can teach classes on how to use a smartphone to do basic tasks. But we can also offer classes on using the voice-activated virtual assistants that come with these devices. We can offer a class on using mobile devices to connect to the library and teach how to download and use each mobile app that we offer.

Next Steps for Digital Inclusion

This chapter really just scratches the surface on the issue of digital inclusion. What's next for a library? A good place to start is to read up on the issues surrounding digital inclusion. Some places to start include the following:

- Pew Research Center's Internet and Technology section. You'll find national statistics and issues surrounding technology trends and digital inclusion needs.
- National Digital Inclusion Alliance. This organization is working to close the digital divide.
- The American Library Association's Digital Literacy page. This page offers links to other websites that focus on digital literacy and inclusion.

Pew Research Center, Internet and Technology
https://www.pewresearch.org/Internet/

National Digital Inclusion Alliance
https://www.digitalinclusion.org

American Library Association's Digital Literacy page
https://literacy.ala.org/digital-literacy/

At your own library, start by simply asking customers what they need. See if your local municipality or a local nonprofit organization has done a local digital inclusion survey of needs.

Once you find out what customers need, see if you can start helping to meet those needs. For example, if your customers need basic internet connectivity, see if you can offer Wi-Fi hot spots for checkout. Maybe your library's customers have adequate internet connectivity, but they want more training on how to better use their mobile devices. If that's the case, you can ramp up a technology training program. Once you have some of these basics figured out, you are ready to map ways to help meet your customers' technology needs.

Notes

1. Joyce Winslow, "America's Digital Divide," *Trust Magazine*, Pew, July 26, 2019, https://www.pewtrusts.org/en/trust/archive/summer-2019/americas-digital-divide.
2. Winslow, "America's Digital Divide."
3. Wikipedia, s.v. "Digital Divide," last updated August 17, 2020, https://en.wikipedia.org/wiki/Digital_divide.
4. "Definitions," National Digital Inclusion Alliance, accessed August 17, 2020, https://www.digitalinclusion.org/definitions.
5. Definitions," National Digital Inclusion Alliance.
6. Digital Literacy," American Library Association, accessed August 17, 2020, https://literacy.ala.org/digital-literacy/.
7. "Computer Laptop Check-Out Policy," Kings County Library, accessed August 31, 2020, https://www.kingscountylibrary.org/computer-laptop-check-out-policy.
8. "Wireless Hotspots," Dekalb Library, accessed November 12, 2020, https://dekalblibrary.org/using-the]-library/computers/wireless-hotspots.
9. Jill Joplin, "Libraries Are Helping Bridge the Digital Divide during COVID-19," *Google Fiber* (blog), April 24, 2020, https://fiber.google.com/blog/2020/libraries-are-helping-bridge-the-digital-divide-during-covid-19.
10. DigitalInclusionKC home page, accessed August 31, 2020, https://digitalinclusionkc.org.
11. "Virtual Reality Arrive in California Libraries," California State Library, accessed November 15, 2020, https://www.library.ca.gov/Content/pdf/pressreleases/Virtual_Reality_Release.pdf.

Chapter 5

Staff Use of Mobile

This final chapter of this report covers how mobile technology and tools can benefit library staff, including providing smartphones and tablets for staff, using mobile devices for outside library events, using mobile devices for video and social media, creating a photo booth for customers, and using tablets as digital signage, catalog kiosks, and exhibit accessories. Staff-focused mobile apps are also discussed.

Smartphones as Staff Tools

Most likely, the great majority of your library workers own smartphones. But in my office, I have a normal desk phone. Can a smartphone replace office phones?

Yes, it (mostly) can. The one thing a smartphone doesn't handle in quite the same way is the conference-calling feature. With my large office phone, it's easy to gather a couple of people around my desk for a quick conference call. That could certainly work using a smartphone, but it would be harder to hear.

Otherwise, a smartphone can definitely work for a work phone. My library's Mitel VoIP phone system comes with mobile app phone software that can turn a smartphone into a phone on our network. So if I wanted to, I could load the app on my personal device and use that as a work phone when I'm away from my desk. This would allow me to get work-related calls that would ring through the mobile app rather than coming through the normal phone functionality of my smartphone.

At my library, we still use desk phones in many places (as in my office) where they make sense. But we also use smartphones (iPhones, to be specific) in some areas, with the Mitel Communicator app loaded onto the phone:

- most of our service desks
- at our new curbside pickup service
- maintenance staff phones
- security staff phones
- the evening and weekend manager shared phone
- bookmobiles and other vehicle-based services that go offsite (They use smartphones for communicating to the library and calling customers.)

Besides the phone app, we also use the Zello app (figure 5.1), which is a push-to-talk app. Zello is basically an app-based walkie-talkie replacement. A little history here: sometime before I started at the library in 2006, the library used actual shortwave walkie-talkie radios that we purchased from the county. They actually covered the whole county, which was more than we really needed. We used these throughout the building—to call for maintenance, security, and digital services. Each service desk had one, and staff often used them instead of calling on the phone or sending an e-mail.

> *Zello*
> https://zello.com

Useful? Definitely. Overkill? Definitely. When we discovered we could replace this system with an app on a smartphone, we did just that and haven't looked back. The mobile app works just as well as the walkie-talkies did and costs us much less per year.

Downsides to Smartphones for Staff

There are certainly some downsides to using a smartphone as your work or service desk phone. For example, smartphones are easy to misplace. They are also easy to steal. Both have happened since my library moved to smartphones. Thankfully, our digital services department can lock the phones remotely if needed.

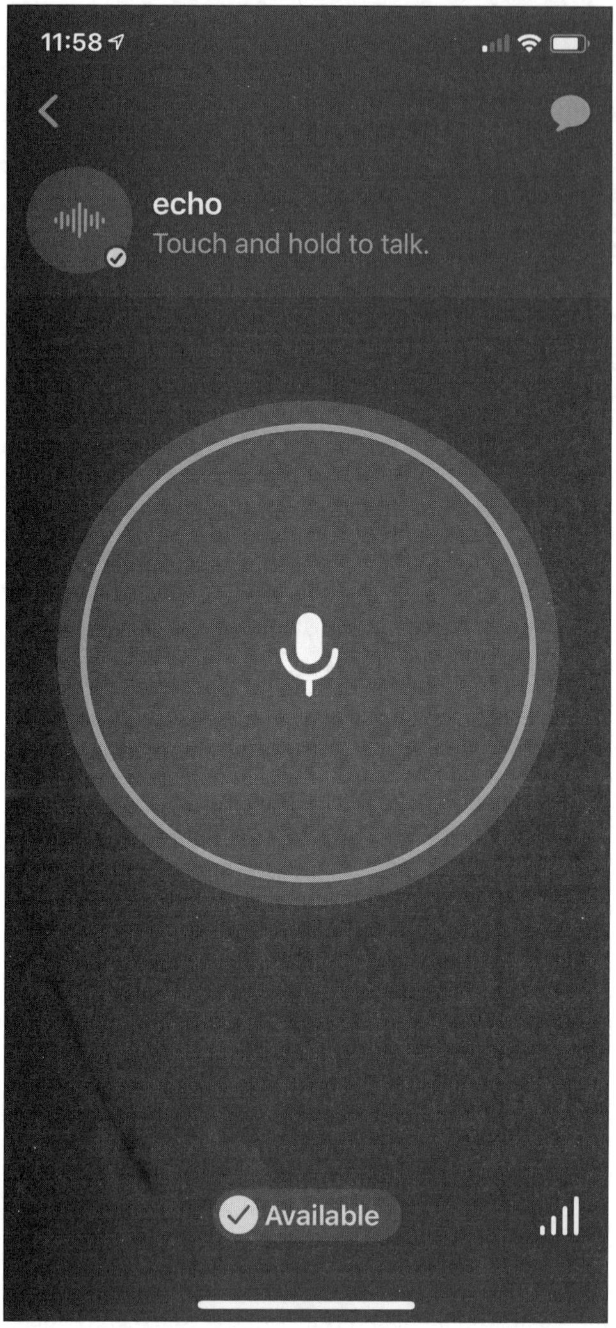

Figure 5.1
Zello app on a smartphone

Panic buttons are another challenge for us. We used to have more stationary service desks in the building (like a large reference desk). Each service desk had a large red panic button that alerted security if help was needed at a specific service desk location.

We have recently moved to smaller service desks and have more staff moving around the building, actively helping customers as needed. Where do you put a panic button in those instances? Thankfully, Zello offers a panic button option. We are in the process of testing that solution and will move to it if it meets our needs.

There are many other types of panic button replacement options that connect directly into phones, are app-based, or are independent of a phone. It's important for staff to be able to discreetly alert security personnel or managers when there's an issue that is escalating.

Tablets in the Library

There are a couple of different ways for library staff to use a tablet: I'll call these customer-facing tablets and staff helps.

Customer-Facing Tablets

There are many ways staff can use a tablet to connect with and help customers. When a customer uses a library tablet, we'll call that a "customer-facing tablet." Here are a few ways that Topeka & Shawnee County Public Library has used iPads over the years:

- *Tablets as catalog kiosks.* In our youth services section of the library, we have set up an iPad on a stand. It points to our library catalog and is meant to be used for quick catalog searches. I see customers using it all the time. The nice thing about this setup is that it's easily movable to anywhere in the building. It just needs power (no wired network cable needed). We can place it closer to the bookshelves than a traditional library catalog computer station, so it's closer to the point of need.
- *Tablets for kids.* We have also experimented with placing a couple of iPads in our youth services area loaded with age-appropriate apps. These were for children to explore and use. We also purchased large, padded iPad cases for the iPads, so if they were dropped, they were less likely to break.
- *Photo booth tablets.* We have used an iPad as a photo booth for the public. We purchased a photo booth app, set the iPad on a stand, and created a fun backdrop with props. We have done this a few times, and people find it to be a fun addition to a library event. It's set up so that you can e-mail or text message the photo to yourself for posting to your own social media accounts. We encourage the use of specific #hashtags depending on the event, such as #summerreading for our summer reading events, or #topekalibrary for a more general hashtag. Then, we can track the photos that customers share in their social media accounts so that we can see and share the photos, too (with permission, of course!).

Figure 5.2
iPads for art event

- *Tablet as art exhibit accessory.* We have used iPads as part of our art gallery exhibits a couple of times. As I write this, we have some iPads set up with art creation apps as part of our Story Worlds interactive children's art exhibit.[1] We have also used iPads in the past for music-related and space-related exhibits (figure 5.2).
- *Tablets as digital signage.* Our public meeting rooms all have iPads as digital signs. We use the Communico Broadcast app for all our digital signage needs. We also use iPads for signing up for our group study rooms (we call them team rooms) and use Communico's Reserve app to manage that process.

Staff Helps

There are also many ways for a library staff member to use tablets for work and for customer interaction:

- *Design tools.* Our graphic designers use iPad design tools to help with graphic design projects.
- *Note-taking tools.* Staff with iPads use them to take notes at meetings, using a variety of note-taking apps. One popular app we use is the GoodNotes app.
- *Public service staff tools.* When a staff member is assigned roving reference duty, they have the option to use an iPad to look up answers to questions, help sign people in to our group study rooms, and so on. It's a little easier on the eyes than a smaller smartphone, and it is much easier to carry around than a laptop.
- *Event sign-up.* We have used iPads, equipped with a Wi-Fi hot spot, to sign people up at parks and other locations for summer reading and other library-related events.

GoodNotes
https://www.goodnotes.com/

Laptops as Mobile Devices

One other point to remember is this: a laptop, though it is not as small as a smartphone or tablet, is also a mobile device. Laptops are also relatively easy to move around. My library has just migrated all of our management staff from desktop-based computers to a laptop-based system with dual monitors and a docking station.

This way, managers have the freedom to take our full desktop system with us to a meeting or to a quiet place to get some work done. We also have the option to work from home should the need arise. Next up for us is to identify other staff who might need the ability to be flexible with where work gets done and to move those staff to a similar laptop-based system.

Social Media Works Best on Mobile

While we are talking about staff use of mobile devices, we need to mention the work of social media in libraries. To properly "do" social media, you really need a smartphone. Social media tools such as Facebook, Instagram, or Twitter all have website versions of their social media channels, but for the most part social media is focused on app-based usage.

Social media apps are designed to work well with smartphones. Many apps use smartphone notification features to send alerts to users. If the app uses location data, it might share who or what you are close to. Some apps allow you to tag a recent photo with information about where the photo was taken or who is included in the photo.

For a library, loading social media apps onto a staff mobile device is pretty handy. This system allows you to interact with your digital customers, even while working the physical floor at the library. If you answer questions via Twitter or Facebook direct messages, you can do real reference work from that phone and help digital library customers at the point of need.

The downside? You need to allow staff to use personal devices to connect to work-related things, or you need to purchase staff-only mobile devices. Staff might not like connecting personal devices to do library-related work. Staff might wonder if the library should help pay for or reimburse them for the phone, or provide a library phone, since it's being used for library work. There are definitely a lot of considerations when asking staff to use mobile devices for library work.

Video Works Great with Mobile

These days, there are many ways to capture video that can be shared on social media sites such as YouTube or Facebook. You might use a mirrorless or DSLR camera. You might have a smaller point-and-shoot camera that captures decent quality video. You might have a bunch of detachable camera lenses and microphones to accessorize your camera and enhance the production quality of the video.

There are, however, extra steps to transfer that video to a social media site. And these days, most of your staff have a full HD-quality, 1080p video recorder in their pockets. Today's smartphone captures truly quality video (figure 5.3).

If you want to start creating videos to share on social media and on your website, start with the camera that's already in your hand—your smartphone. After a while, if you want to improve the quality of your videos, you may want to think about accessorizing your smartphone with some additional tools. For example, you can purchase microphones made for your mobile devices that will improve the quality of the audio for your videos. You can also buy lens attachments that extend the functionality of your mobile device's camera lens. You can buy handheld smartphone video stabilizers that will help remove the extra shake from your videos.

Better lighting will definitely help too! There are lots of inexpensive video-focused lighting systems that work great with smartphone-based video systems.

So, get your phone out, press Record, and start experimenting with video!

Wi-Fi Hot Spots for Staff Use

One important thing you will need for effective mobile device use is a good, strong Wi-Fi signal. You can get that with a data plan, certainly. You can also ensure a strong signal if you have robust Wi-Fi in your library building. One easy way to get a good Wi-Fi signal when outside of your library building is to use mobile Wi-Fi hot spots.

Mobile Wi-Fi hot spots connect to the internet without having to use a smartphone's data plan and a potentially spotty signal. In Shawnee County, as I mentioned before, mobile connectivity varies greatly as you move into more rural areas of the county.

My library has used hot spots for our bookmobiles for years. This allows us to do two things: first, we use hot spots for checking items out to customers. This allows us to do checkout in real time, because the laptops on our bookmobiles can connect directly back to the ILS located in our data center.

Second, we have a separate hot spot designated for customer use. This plan allows our customers to get

Figure 5.3
David making a video with his iPhone

help downloading e-books or using something on our website without having to use their data plan.

Another new service that we are hoping to test soon is our new book bike! This recent purchase will be loaded with books to check out and will be parked in various places around town. The staff member assigned to book bike duty will have an iPad and a hot spot to connect to the web, help with checkout, or answer questions as needed.

Mobile Apps

I have mentioned a variety of mobile apps that my library uses on our mobile devices. Here's a list for your reference:

- *Zello:* This is our walkie-talkie replacement app.
- *Paycom:* We use Paycom for our payroll software. There's an app-based version for checking your pay stub and for clocking in and out.
- *GoodNotes:* This is one of the note-taking apps we like on an iPad.
- *Patron database apps:* Many apps can be included here, including OverDrive, Libby, Hoopla, Flipster, EBSCOhost, RBdigital, Creativebug, and Lynda. These days, many library databases have an app-based version of the service.
- *Microsoft Office 365 apps:* We recently moved to Microsoft 365, and Microsoft has app-based versions of its Office suite of products.
- *Photo booth apps:* We use a variety of apps for photo booth fun.
- *Kiosk mode apps:* We use Kiosk Pro Lite and Kiosk Mode apps for our digital signage. They place the iPad in kiosk mode so no one can get into the app and mess things up.
- *Mitel Connect:* This is the app-based version of our Mitel VoIP phone system.
- *Basecamp:* This is the app version of the project management tool we use.
- *Communico Engage:* We use Communico's mobile app as our library-wide mobile app. This app searches our catalog, works as a calendar of events, and lets us place a variety of other information from our website onto the mobile app for quick lookup (such as our hours).

I hope you have seen throughout this publication that mobile devices have a great many uses for a library system, both as customer-facing and as staff-facing tools. Helping customers connect with the library by using your library's mobile apps can be a great help for customers on the go, as well as providing convenience and comfort to use the apps on their devices anywhere in your building.

Note

1. "Story Worlds," Topeka & Shawnee County Public Library, accessed September 4, 2020, https://tscpl.org/gallery/story-worlds.

Notes

Notes

Library Technology REPORTS

Upcoming Issues	
April 57:3	**Video Accessibility** by Carli Spina
May/June 57:4	**Creating Adaptable Digital Preservation Workflows** by Erin Baucom
July 57:5	**Metadata Applications Profiles for Library Data** by Jeremy Myntti, Theo Gerontakos, and Ben Riesenberg